A Birthday Is a Magic Day

A Birthday Is a Magic Day

By Dean Walley

Illustrations by
Alice Ann Biggerstaff
Lettering by
Mary Ann Odom

HALLMARK EDITIONS

Copyright © by Hallmark Cards Inc.,
Kansas City, Missouri. All Rights Reserved.
Printed in the United States of America.
Library of Congress Catalog Card Number: 79-94567
Standard Book Number: 87529-022-1

A Birthday Is a Magic Day

Whether you are grown up...

Or very, very small...

A birthday is a magic day--
Your finest day of all.

It's the day you said
"Hello World!"

The first day you were you...

A magic day for wishing on
And seeing dreams come true...

It's a wake-up-extra early day
When you shout,

"My birthday's here!"

A wear-a-great-big smile day
You've waited for all year.

And when people ask,
"How old are you?"
Now you can wink and say....

"*Why I'm a whole year older
Than I was yesterday.*"

*A birthday is a magic day
That has a way of bringing
Happy things that make you feel
Like laughing...*

Dancing...

And that very special magic
Will remind your
favorite friends
To drop a line...

*Or drop on by
Before your birthday ends.*

The games...

And the surprises...

Plus the things you
love to eat,
Are all part of the magic
That makes
your day complete.

Yes, a birthday is a

Magic

Day

*If you're small,
It's a feel-tall day...*

❊And if you're all grown up,
It's a pleasant-to-recall day ❊

*And whether you are young or old
You're sure to find a part*

Of that special

Birthday

Magic

Stays on within your heart.